WICCA

for

Self-transformation

WICCA
for
Self-transformation
Use magic to
transform your life

MARIE BRUCE

SIRIUS

SIRIUS

This edition published in 2023 by Sirius Publishing, a division of
Arcturus Publishing Limited,
26/27 Bickels Yard, 151–153 Bermondsey Street,
London SE1 3HA

All images courtesy of Shutterstock

ISBN: 978-1-3988-2613-7
AD010761UK

Printed in China

Contents

Introduction

Welcome, Changeling

Step into the silver shadows of self-transformation, where a powerful new life of magical possibility awaits you. As enchanted creatures, changelings are capable of shape-shifting transformations, but you need not belong to the fairy realms for such magic. Within your own life, you can transform yourself into whatever you want to be, achieving success and accomplishments along the way. For in the world of magic and witchcraft, we are *all* changelings.

Each of us has our own path to tread through life, our own goals and talents, skills and experiences. We also have our own habits, quirks and behaviour, which may or may not be beneficial to us. In this book, we are going to explore how change actually works and how to harness its inevitable power so that the changes you face are largely self-driven, rather than nasty surprises that pull the rug out from under you. Because, if you allow yourself to stagnate for too long, rest assured

that a major life change will come along to shake you out of your comfort zone! But why wait for that? Why not take charge of the changes you *want* to make and start driving your life in the direction of your dreams, so that you live a charmed existence on a day-to-day basis?

It is possible to live a charmed life, but you have to believe it in order for it to become your new reality. Witches know that the visions they carry in their minds are exactly what their subconscious will manifest, so to bring about a positive change, one must maintain a positive attitude—sometimes in very difficult circumstances. However, there are spells, rituals and tools to help you maintain your vision of a positive future and, throughout the course of this book, you will learn how to support your ambitions for a transformed life in a magical way, because this is where the future of your dreams begins!

Serene blessings,

Marie Bruce x

CHAPTER ONE

In the Silver Shadows, Where Dreams Begin

W e live in a world where we are frequently told that anything is possible, but when the odds seem stacked against you, it can be hard to believe that this is true. Many people work long hours for low pay, their time devoured by a job that provides no more than the basic necessities, leaving little left over to turn ambitions into reality. Some people work several jobs yet still struggle to make ends meet. In such situations, being told that you have the power to change your life can feel almost insulting, yet learning how to see past your current circumstances is the first step to achieving any goal.

For some people, ambition is an alien concept—something other people might have, but not them. They do not feel entitled to dream, to set goals or to hold onto ambitions long enough to achieve them. This might be because they have never been taught how aspiration actually works. So they aim too high to begin with and quickly become disheartened. They might even have been told off as youngsters for day-dreaming, thereby quashing their skill for aspiration, rather than nurturing it. This is exactly what happened to Michael Flatley, the creator of the hit Irish dance show, *Lord of the Dance*. He was frequently told to stop day-dreaming and pay more attention in school. However, the things he was fantasizing about as a child became his reality in adulthood, because he didn't let go of his dream. He went on to create the top-selling dance show in history. Dreams are powerful things.

The fact is, day-dreaming is good for you. Not only does it provide an escape from the workaday world, it can give your higher self (that part of you that is in contact with divine energy) a chance to communicate and show you what you are truly capable of achieving if you set your mind to it. It can help you to create goals and encourages you to think in terms of possibility, rather than limitation. Dreams are signs that you are capable of more. They light the path to productivity and achievement. They are the seeds of success and you won't get very far without them. Fortunately, your dreams are always waiting in the wings and all you have to do is invite them to take centre stage in your life.

What is Self-Transformation?

Self-transformation is the art of turning your dreams into your reality. It is the thought process needed to start making positive changes in your life. It comprises small, incremental steps that lead to a big transformation in your daily experience. When we talk about self-transformation, we are referring to a deliberate process of self-directed change. It could involve developments in your career, romantic attachments, finances, and so on. It could mean all of the above.

Working on one aspect of your life at a time usually yields the best results. When you have achieved the transformation you want in that area, you can

move on to the next. The trick to success is to focus on one thing only, beginning with the area that bothers you the most. So, if you hate your current job but you're happy to be single for a while, then begin to transform your working life. Once you have the results you want in that area, then move on to transforming your romantic life too. In this way you can transform your whole life, step-by-step, giving your entire focus to a single area, before moving on to the next. As you work through this book, you may find it helpful to have a notebook and pen handy, so that you are prepared for the exercises as they come up.

Think Like a Changeling

In folklore, changelings are powerful creatures of the fairy realms who move among humans unnoticed. They are magical beings who can cast spells and perform rituals to ensure they live their best life in the human world. You can harness the changeling's powers, using magic and spell-casting to tailor your life so that it fits well and suits you perfectly. Your life is not set in stone and nor are you. Both are malleable and can be reshaped and molded until they are exactly what you want. Everything is subject to change, so think like a changeling and be the force who directs the transformation to your own liking. Remember…

✦ You have the power to change.

✦ You have the power to transform your life.

✦ You get to decide how you want your journey to progress.

✦ Stagnation is a choice—but so is growth. Choose wisely.

✦ Each day is a new beginning.

✦ It's never too late to change.

✦ Your past does not need to determine your future.

✦ Your future is yours to create!

Wiccan Tools of Transformation

Witches know how to change their lives for the better. We use magic and spells to hone our focus on what we want to achieve. We release negative thought patterns and self-sabotaging habits that get in our way and we can frequently be found meditating on visualizations of our glorious future! Visualizations and affirmations are some of the most powerful tools in the art of self-transformation, largely because you can use them anywhere and no one else will know what you are doing.

You can find a quiet space in the middle of the working day to close your eyes and visualize your dream job. You can change your passwords so that they become affirmations of your goals, using keywords and phrases such as "work from home" or "rural life" in order to draw those things closer to you and manifest them. You can use a wallpaper on your phone or computer that illustrates your goal. These are very subtle, yet extremely powerful acts of magic that witches use to manifest their goals and dreams. You will find affirmations and visualizations, as well as spells, rituals and exercises, throughout this book to help you bring about the kind of transformations you are aiming for. Let's begin with an exercise to determine what your current circumstances are and how much transformation is required.

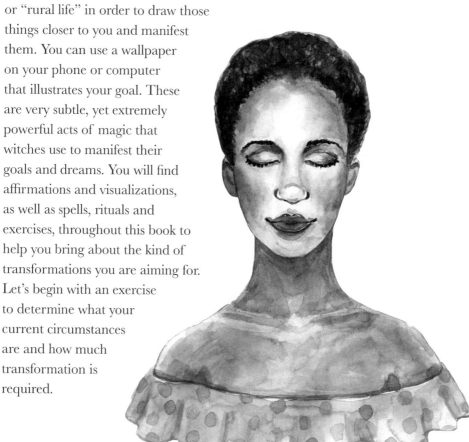

Where Are You Now?

Before the journey of self-transformation can begin, you need to take stock of your life to see where you are unhappy and what requires the most work. Take a notepad and pen and make a list of all the areas of your life that you can think of. Give each area a score from one to ten, with one meaning that you are very unhappy in this area and ten meaning that you are extremely satisfied with it. Here are some examples to get you started, but feel free to create your own list:

- Work/career
- Finances
- Family
- Romantic relationships
- Hobbies/sports
- Holidays/travel
- Creativity

- Study/learning
- Independence/autonomy
- Spirituality
- Self-care
- Body-image and fitness
- Free time
- Socializing

Next go through the list to see which areas of your life you want to work on first. These should be the ones that have the lowest score, which you are the most dissatisfied with. Pick one of these areas and use that as your main focus as you work through the rest of this book. This is the journey of transformation you need to prioritize. Once you have transformed this area of your life, you can repeat the process with the next lowest score on the list and so on, thereby transforming every aspect of your life that requires attention, over a period of time. Bear in mind that self-transformation isn't instantaneous and it is never truly complete. It is a process that will require continuous effort on your part, which is why it is better to focus only on one area at a time. Trying to change your entire life in one go would be far too overwhelming.

Seeing Is Believing

Visualization is one of the most powerful tools you can use for self-transformation. The subconscious can't tell the difference between a fantasy and reality. It simply magnetizes whatever you focus on the most, which is why when you worry about debt, you attract more money problems. We all have the ability to visualize things, though many people waste this valuable skill by imagining worst-case scenarios. If you can picture your front door, you can visualize. It really is as simple as that, so try not to overthink the concept.

In magic, we make a habit of imagining the *best* possible outcome instead, knowing that what we think, we attract. Magical visualization means picturing the change you want to see, as if it has already happened and you are enjoying the results. You will notice that the more you do this, the more your emotions will respond to the visualization and you may begin to smile at the vision and experience joy. This is a sign that you are changing your outlook on life and seeing a better future for yourself. It means that the transformation has begun at a deep emotional level, so keep at it and notice any subtle signs of manifestation. When you visualize your goal on a daily basis, your behaviour will also begin to shift so that it is more in alignment with the vision. Your behaviour creates habits and it is your habits that create your day-to-day life experience.

If you wanted to gain a promotion at work, for example, and you were visualizing that every day, you might begin to take greater care over the job you are currently doing, or dress more smartly, or spend more time chatting with the boss about your hopes for new opportunities. Over time, these shifts in behaviour should be noticed and could lead to the promotion you have been visualizing—thus the transformation is complete.

TRANSFORMATIONAL TOOL: VISUALIZATION MADE EASY

The best time to visualize is when you are nice and relaxed, so the ideal times are when you are lying in bed just before you go to sleep and as soon as you wake up. Close your eyes and spend from five to ten minutes visualizing your goal. You might picture yourself in your dream job, at your goal weight, publishing your book, walking down the aisle on your wedding day or building a successful business. Imagine what achieving your goal would feel like and how it would benefit you and those around you. Whatever your goal of self-transformation is, visualize it as if it has already happened, for ten minutes every morning and evening. Because once you can *see* it clearly, you can start to believe it is possible for you to *achieve* it. And that is when the magic happens!

TRANSFORMATIONAL TOOL: PASSWORD POWER

Many people use passwords every day, to log in at work or to open their phone or laptop, so why not make this simple daily routine work for you by turning your passwords into affirmations. Using words of power as your passwords means that you are reminding yourself and the universe of what you want, on a daily basis. This is such an easy thing to do and it really does work. Make sure your passwords reflect your goal of self-transformation, so if you want to start a business, use the name of your business as your password. If you want to achieve a particular exercise goal or revamp your image, use a password which reflects this, such as "perfectly fit" or "smarten up". Reset your passwords today and let the power of affirming your goal each day work its magic.

TRANSFORMATIONAL TOOL: BACKGROUND DREAMS

Use your computer desktop background as a vision board to help attract your dreams. Simply find an image, collage or inspirational quote that matches your goal and set this as your wallpaper background. You can even use websites to create a digital vision board, if you prefer. In this way you will be reminded of your goal every time you open up your laptop or phone.

CHAPTER TWO:

Change and Change About

We are frequently told that change is hard. While that might be true to an extent, change is as necessary as the air we breathe, hence the old adage "a change is as good as a rest". The truth is that change is inevitable and the sooner you make peace with that, the easier it will be when life takes an unexpected turn.

Change can be a scary prospect, which is why people are often content to remain stuck in a rut. Familiarity provides a comfort zone. This is fine if you are totally happy with all aspects of your life but, for most of us, there is at least one area that could use some attention—whether it be work, love or finances. Positive change usually starts internally, in that you must decide what you want and set goals to achieve it. A wish list simply isn't strong enough, because it assumes that positive change is something handed to you on a plate. If you sit back and wait for all your dreams to just come to you, you will still be waiting for them in your dotage! You have to be the one to go out and achieve them.

Reinventing yourself and your life is a challenging process. It won't happen overnight and you must commit fully to the development. Don't worry if you can't see all the steps you have to take to achieve the life you want. Not being able to see your way ahead is all part of the process and while it can be nerve-racking, it doesn't mean that you are bound to fail or that you shouldn't take the initial steps towards change. Have faith in your own capabilities and trust that you are being guided to a new career or a more fulfilling relationship. Seek out a new adventure and reinvent yourself along the way. The following ritual will help you to visualize the new you.

A SPELL TO REINVENT YOURSELF

Moon phase: Full moon for greatest power.
You will need: A pen and notepad, a tealight and holder, a stick of your favourite incense and holder.

Light the candle and incense and settle down with the notepad and pen. Think of one area of your life you want to reinvent. Write down how you want to bring about a positive change and how you can reinvent yourself to manifest the goal—for example, if you want a new relationship, you could begin to dress more attractively day-to-day, or contact an old flame to rekindle the spark. Write a detailed account of what you need to do—the simple steps you can begin to take right away to reinvent yourself. Now repeat the mantra below nine times:

"Day by day, each step I take, I move towards the dream life I make."

Repeat this mantra daily to remind you of your goal and place the list of changes you need to make somewhere you will see it every day. Remember that positive change takes time and you must shake off the old to make way for the new.

SHEDDING AN OLD SKIN

Reinventing yourself often involves releasing the old you. You will need to let go of all the old patterns that are not in alignment with the person you want to become. This could mean changing your routines, your style or your career. It might mean letting go of bad habits that can sabotage your successful transformation. If your goal is to become financially stable, for example, you will need to break the habit of acquiring debt, or overspending. If you want to develop a good work ethic, you will need to stop arriving late at the office. Transformation of any kind usually means letting go of something that is standing in your way. You must shed the old skin in order to show off your bright new colours.

TRANSFORMATIONAL TOOL: DECLUTTER YOUR LIFE

Believe it or not, decluttering your belongings is a great way to get the ball rolling. Letting go of all the possessions that no longer suit you—or which remind you of who you used to be—is a good exercise in kick-starting the transformation. It makes a space for the new you to step into. It allows room for personal growth.

Mentally divide your home into sections and declutter one at a time, working through the whole house over a period of days or weeks. Try to begin with the section which reflects your self-transformation target, so if you are wanting to change your image, begin with your wardrobe. Likewise, if you want to improve your financial life, go through your bank statements, credit agreements and so on, and make payment plans

that put you on track to greater stability. Take your unwanted items to a charity shop, or sell them online, so that someone else can use and appreciate them. As you bag up your old things chant the following mantra to help with the process.

"Transformation is the key, I say goodbye to the old me,
I shed this skin and let it go, new brighter colours I now show."

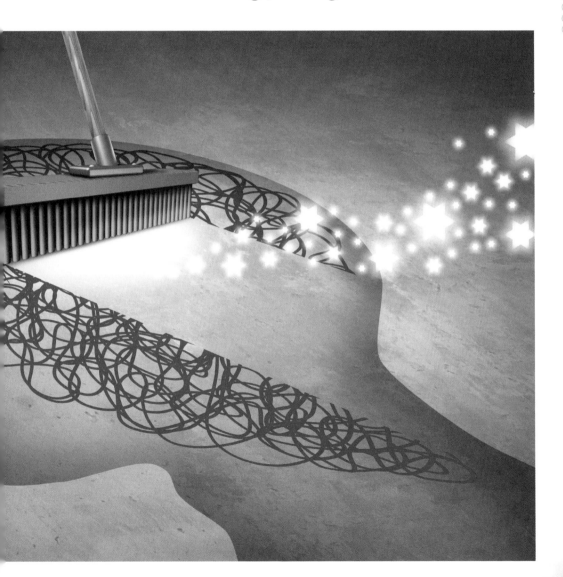

The Science of Change

In a nutshell, self-transformation is about habits. It is about identifying those you need to break and designing the new ones you need to make, in order to improve your life. Change is absolutely *always* possible—it doesn't matter if you have been stuck in a rut for a decade—but it isn't easy. You will need to be completely dedicated to your new way of life and this involves developing a new way of thinking and behaving.

Transformation isn't a matter of luck. There is a science behind change and the science states that it takes between 21 and 30 days to break a habit. It is also true that it is easier to break a habit if you immediately replace it with a new one, rather than leaving a void, but it takes approximately 66 days for this new habit to become an automatic behaviour, meaning that for 66 days you will need to remind yourself to pick up the *new* habit and not fall back on the old one. Now, while the initial 30 days of habit-breaking doesn't *seem* like a long time, to a smoker or drinker trying to quit, it can feel like a lifetime! This is why many people fall off the wagon or light up a cigarette after two weeks—because it's hard work. The good news is that, if you can make it past the 30-day mark, it becomes much easier.

How does this link in with self-transformation? Well, because the science of change can be applied to anything, so if your goal is to become a novelist, you would need to make a new habit of writing so many words a day for 66 days, by which time you will have formed the habit of a writer. If you constantly spend money, but your goal is to achieve financial stability and savings, you would need to stop shopping for a minimum of 30 days, while depositing money into a savings account instead for a minimum of 66 days. In this way, the buzz you once got from online shopping is now brought about by seeing the balance of your savings increase, and all you've done is switch out an old habit for a new one. This is how transformation unfolds.

Identifying Your Habits

You will need to identify which of your daily habits need to change, in order to facilitate the transformation you require. Some habits are so subtle that we don't even acknowledge them as such. Watching dramas on television every night is a common pastime in many households, but if you add up how many hours a week you spend this way, you will soon see why you can't find the time to write a book or start a business. Take a close look at your life and try to identify the habits you currently indulge in and whether they are in alignment with your goal or not. If not, think about what new habit you need to develop, not only to replace the old one, but also to draw you closer to achieving your transformational target. If you want to lose weight, for example, you might need to replace the habit of picking up fast food on your way home from work, with the new one of going to the gym instead and eating something healthier after working out.

What new habits do you need to develop? And what new daily routines can you put in place that will bring your dream life one step closer? Use the science of change to your advantage and remember that transformation is a natural aspect of life. Growth is good and leaving the past behind is all part of the journey. Any degree of transformation begins on the inside with your habits, behaviour and mindset, so begin to release the old you right now using the spell below.

A SPELL TO RELEASE OLD HABITS

Moon phase: Waning to draw the habit away.

Items required: sticky notes, a pen, a small cauldron or heat-proof dish, a lighter.

At the time of the waning moon, gather the items together and spend a few moments reflecting on the habit you need to break. Think about how it has affected your life so far and how it might be holding you back. Imagine yourself free of this habit and commit to the 30-day rule of breaking it, starting today. Now write down the habit on a sticky note, fold the note in half, set light to the end and drop it into the cauldron to burn, saying:

> *"A bad habit burns within this fire,*
> *To be free of it is my desire,*
> *As it burns, I let it go.*
> *And a brand new me I come to know."*

You can repeat this spell each day for the 30-day period, or whenever you feel tempted to fall back on the old habit. If you do return to the habit, simply start the process again from day one.

CHAPTER THREE

Self-Analysis is the Key

Transformation requires patience. It will not happen overnight, but that is because you need time to reinvent a whole new you and a new way of life. Many people allow circumstances, and the people they are close to, to shape them and to define who they are. With self-transformation, it is down to you, and you alone, to determine who you are going to be and the kind of life you will lead. This process involves a certain amount of self-analysis. You need to know how—and why—you want this change, how you might fail, and what or who might stand in your way.

Sources of Change

If change is natural, then why is it so hard? Good question. The answer is that, as humans, we are hard-wired to avoid pain, so anything that is outside of our comfort zone becomes challenging. The trouble is that we can get extremely comfortable with things that are bad for us, which is why people often remain in jobs and relationships that are harmful to their mental and physical health. Think about the bullied employee who stays in their job, because the idea of starting again elsewhere is just too challenging. That uncomfortable situation has, ironically, become their comfort zone, which is why they stay.

This is something you need to be aware of and to avoid if possible. Comfort zones are all well and good, until they start to work against you. You need to be brave enough to step outside of your comfort zone, and even to leave it behind, in some cases. You deserve to live a life you love and, if that's not your current experience, then something needs to change. That said, there are three types of life change everyone has to contend with: self-directed, enforced and unwelcome change.

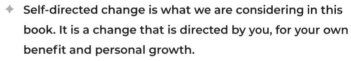

- ✦ **Self-directed change is what we are considering in this book. It is a change that is directed by you, for your own benefit and personal growth.**
- ✦ **Enforced change is the kind that comes from an external influence. It is change you are being forced into making. The external influence could be your job, your family, your finances or the authorities.**
- ✦ **Unwelcome change comes about through an undesirable event, such as a bereavement, redundancy, divorce or a life-altering injury or diagnosis. You haven't been forced into this change by another person as such, but it is beyond your control and unwelcome nonetheless.**

For self-transformation to be effective and lasting, it has to be self-directed change, or a transformation used as a positive response to an unwelcome event, such as those listed on page 33. In short, this means that it has to come from your heart. If you are wanting to make changes because someone close to you thinks you should, then consider very carefully if this is something you *really* want to do, or if you are responding to a subtle variety of coercive control.

TRANSFORMATIONAL TOOL: MISSION STATEMENT

Every journey of transformation must be backed up by a sound motivation. If you do not know *why* you want to make changes in your life, then any transformation is likely to be fleeting, before you revert to your old routines and habits. Take a notebook or journal and, at the top of the first page, write the transformation that you wish to make. Now think about all the reasons why you want to make this change. What are your motivations? What drives you forward on this journey? Do these motivations and driving forces come from you, or someone else? Once you have a clear idea of why this transformation is so important to you, create a mission statement that sums it up and write this underneath the goal.

Here is an example: *"My mission is to create a successful pottery business from my garden shed, so that I can work from home and be there for my children. To achieve this, I will transform myself into a successful creative entrepreneur and business person."*

Now you have a mission statement for your goal. This is a vital part of any kind of transformation, because you have to know where you are going, why you want to get there and what you hope to achieve along the way. Write your own mission statement on a postcard and put it somewhere you will see it every day.

Failure and Sabotage

The next step on your journey of self-transformation is, interestingly, to try and anticipate how and where you might fail. Failure itself is not a bad thing, providing we learn and grow from it. Repeating the same kind of failure over and over again, however, is something to watch out for. In psychotherapy, we call these repeated patterns that lead to failure self-sabotage or maladaptive behaviours. One example of self-sabotage would be someone who is always late for job interviews. They sabotage their chances of getting a new job with their tardiness, which makes a bad first impression on prospective employers.

How might you fail, or sabotage, your chances at transformation? What might you do to underachieve in your goal? While everyone has some self-sabotaging tendencies, learning to identify yours can be the difference between success and failure in reaching your target. Overleaf are some common self-sabotaging behaviours. How many do you relate to?

Note that behaviours marked with an asterisk are the ones society regards as virtues! Be extra careful with these as they are still self-sabotaging techniques.

- **Procrastination** leads to missed deadlines and opportunities.
- **Laziness** brings about the same results as above and also makes a bad impression.
- **Tardiness** means people will just get fed up of waiting for you and move on.
- **Messiness** leads to disorganization, lost documents, a bad image and so on.
- ***Perfectionism**—remember done is better than perfect! Just let it go.
- **Negative self-talk** can mean you talk yourself out of success and achievement.
- **Envy** puts the focus on what others are doing rather than what you are achieving yourself.
- **Narcissism**—thinking too well of yourself means you might wait for everything to be handed to you on a plate. It won't be!
- **Substance abuse**—you can't achieve anything if you are lost in a mental haze.
- **Drains**—including gambling, shopping, pornography and internet scrolling—misdirect your time, energy and money.
- ***Selflessness/martyrdom** can mean you are living entirely for other people with no life of your own.

Learning to identify the moment you move into self-sabotaging behaviours is crucial, because then you can nip it in the bud before it derails your plans completely. While it isn't always easy to admit that you can be your own worst enemy, ignoring the fact only leads to the eventual collapse of your plans, so it is much better to be honest with yourself and keep a check on self-sabotaging behaviours so that they don't get out of hand.

Who Keeps You Small?

Along with self-sabotage, you should also bear in mind the possibility that other people might try to sabotage your chances of success too. As unsavoury as it is to think about, sometimes your nearest and dearest don't *want* you to change. There are lots of reasons why those close to you might try to throw a spanner in the works. It could be that they feel intimidated by the changes you are trying to make, or they might begin to feel inferior in the face of your success. Whatever their reasons, it pays to identify what's happening early on in the process—who might try to keep you small and what their motivations might be for doing so.

Envy is an obvious motivation for someone to try and sabotage your success. If a best friend or sibling is jealous of your achievements, then it is possible that they might attempt to take you down a peg or two. This is not uncommon, sadly. Envy is also the most common motivation for strangers and acquaintances to try and sabotage you too. If someone shows signs of envy towards you, it means they believe that they are more worthy of your success and opportunities than you are, and they might start moving against you with malicious intent. They might even try to take those opportunities away from you and steal them for themselves. This is more likely to be the case with friends/frenemies and strangers than with close family, but it is something to keep in mind. If someone begins sniping at you about your goals and achievements, you would be wise to limit how much information they have about you and your plans. You might need to restrict them on your social media and reduce the amount of time you spend with them.

Of course, not all sabotage is malicious in nature, nor is it deliberate. Parents can often be accidental saboteurs, by making their grown-up children feel guilty for wanting to lead a life of their own. In most cases, this kind of sabotage comes from a place of fear, in that they simply don't want to lose you. This can also be true of romantic partners, too. They might be afraid that your transformation could lead to new opportunities which widen the gap between you and your loved ones. A classic example of this would be the spouse who doesn't want their partner to lose weight because they are afraid it will result in too much attention from rivals. But the fact is no one has the right to keep you small or to limit your life in any way.

A SPELL TO PREVENT SABOTAGE

Moon phase: Full moon.

Items required: A small tub and lid, a piece of card small enough to fit in the tub, black electrical tape, a black pen, water.

This is a classic binding spell, which freezes the negative influence in your life. At the time of the full moon, cast this spell to help prevent any kind of sabotage being used to derail your plans. This could be self-sabotage habits or the sabotage of other people moving against you. Using a black pen, write the nature of the sabotage on the piece of card (for example, laziness or envy). Next, use the tape and wrap it around the whole of the card until it is completely covered. As you do so, say:

> *"All saboteurs I bind within, all self-defeat I keep at bay,*
> *Despite these things I will win, and live my dream from this day."*

Finally, put the card in the tub, fill the tub with water, put on the lid and place it in the freezer. Leave it there until you have completed the transformation, then once you have succeeded, take the tub out of the freezer, allow its contents to melt, then throw away the card. Repeat the spell for every transformation you want to make.

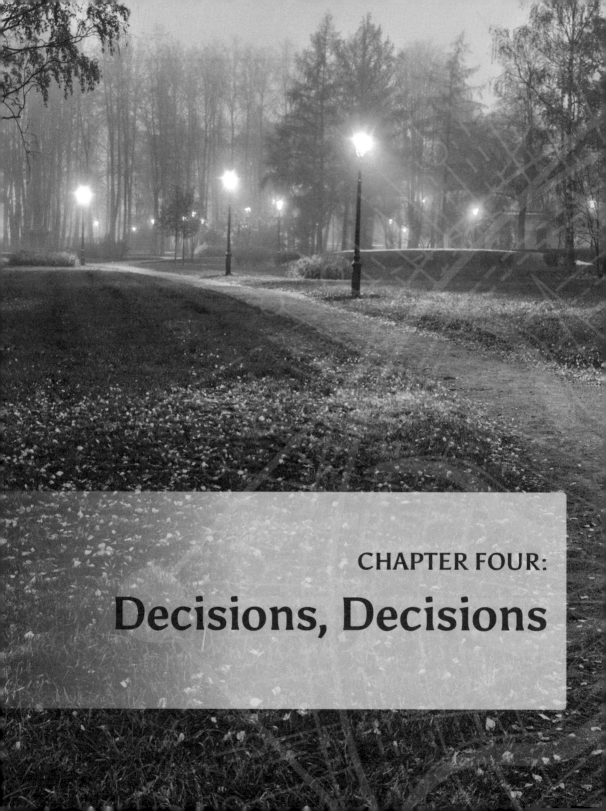

CHAPTER FOUR:
Decisions, Decisions

So far, we have looked at how transformation works and the things that can get in the way. In this chapter you are going to begin making plans for what you want to achieve. By now you should already have your main goal in mind, with a mission statement and daily passwords that support it. You should also be visualizing your goal morning and evening, every day, as if it has already happened. In this chapter

you are going to further stabilize your goal and give it legs. What do we mean by that? Giving legs to your goal means you are providing a structure for success and transformation to take place. It involves deep diving into your psyche to decide who you really want to be, what you want to achieve and designing a life you love.

Transformational Tool: Who Do You Want to Be?

Whenever you ask someone what they want from their life, they will invariably begin by telling you what they *don't* want! They might say things like:

✦ I don't want to be poor and in debt.
✦ I don't want to be stuck in a dead-end job my whole life.
✦ I don't want to be in bad relationship.
✦ I don't want to be single forever.
✦ I don't want to keep drifting through life.
✦ I don't want to be all alone.

Now, while it is important to know exactly what you *don't* want, it is equally important not to dwell on it. Why? Because you attract what you think about the most, so the more you focus on what you don't want, the more you will attract all those things. If this sounds familiar, then you will need to make a significant shift in your mindset.

The good news is that life is all about balance, so for everything you say you don't want, there is an equal and opposite component that you *do* want. Shifting your mindset is simply a case of identifying the opposite component and focusing your mind on that instead. Taking the list above as an example, we can see that the opposite components would read something like this:

✦ I want to be affluent and financially stable.

✦ I want an exciting career that fulfills me.

✦ I want to be in a wonderful, loving relationship.

✦ I want to enjoy a vibrant dating life and meet lots of new people.

✦ I want to maintain a strong sense of direction and personal drive towards my goals

✦ I want to be surrounded by friends who love, respect and support me.

This is a great start, because you have turned the negatives into positives. Now you need to take it one step further by turning the positives into *affirmative* statements of your life, like so:

✦ I AM affluent and financially stable.

✦ I HAVE an exciting career that fulfills me.

✦ I AM in a wonderful, loving relationship.

✦ I DO enjoy a vibrant dating life and meet lots of new people.

✦ I ALWAYS maintain a strong sense of direction and personal drive towards my goals.

✦ I AM surrounded by friends who love, respect and support me.

This is the fastest way to change your mindset from a negative one of limitations and complaint, to a more positive one, which affirms your future by speaking of your goals in the present tense, as if they are already your reality. Whenever you find yourself dwelling on all the things you wish were different, use this process to switch to a more positive mental state, affirming a bright future for yourself and who you want to be.

Design a Life You Love

Have you ever sat down and actually *designed* your life? Have you ever made a five-year plan on paper, or mapped out where you want to be by a certain age? If not, then it's time to make a start! Many people spend time planning weddings, birthday celebrations and so on, but few rarely take the time to sit and commit to planning out their life. They just leave it all to chance. While it's true that you can't plan for every eventuality, if you have no plan at all in place, then you will be buffeted by the whims of fate, so it is far better to take as much control of your life as is humanly possible and that means creating the kind of lifestyle that suits you best.

Creating a life map can be such a fun exercise. Here you get to dream on the page about all the things you would love to do. While you can create a life plan at any time, I believe that it is essential to make one in the months following a big upheaval of some sort or an unwelcome life change, such as bereavement or divorce. Taking charge of your future in this way can become part of the healing process and it helps to start to imagine your way forward. It is also important not to plan too far ahead, as that can be very overwhelming. Stick to five-year plans that you remake every four years. Don't wait until you have achieved everything on your current plan before you make a new one, simply move unachieved goals across to the new five-year life map and take it from there.

TRANSFORMATIONAL TOOL: LIFE MAPPING

To begin with, make a list of all the things you want to experience, do and achieve. Make sure to include all aspects of your life, going back to the list in Chapter One to help you. Next split these goals into three sections, as below:

- ✦ **The immediate goals** you can take on in the next six months.
- ✦ **The intermediate goals** you plan to achieve in the next 12 to 24 months.
- ✦ **The long-range goals** you want to complete in the next five years.

For each section, try to include goals for career, relationships, family, travel, experiences and hobbies. Make sure each section also includes something to achieve, something to do regularly, something to look forward to, a place to visit and something to aim high for. In this way you will remain productive and you will keep up the momentum of your life, enjoying new experiences, rather than falling back into a rut. Be aware that these plans need not be elaborate or expensive. For example, you can choose to go for a walk in the woods or local park every week as your regular goal, or plan to get a pet as an intermediate goal.

TRANSFORMATIONAL TOOL: 66-DAY HABIT TRACKER

The next step is to look at your list of immediate goals on your life map. Choose one of these goals and think about what new habit you would need to create to make that goal a reality. Does this goal align with who you want to be? Will achieving it move you forward in your transformational journey? If it will, then make a commitment to creating a new habit to support the goal. For instance, if you want to learn to play an instrument, make a new habit of daily music practice, alongside weekly lessons. If you want to improve your self-image, make a new habit of taking exercise or planning your outfits the night before so that you are ready to go the next day, knowing that you look great. Repeat and track this new habit for at least 66 days, marking it off in your dairy or on your calendar, until it becomes an automatic behaviour. Then start a new habit. In this way, your day-to-day life will support your transformation.

CAN YOU AIM TOO HIGH?

This is a tricky one. One the one hand, you should aim for the moon. On the other hand, not everyone has what it takes to be an astronaut! Certainly, your shorter-term goals should be the most achievable, because if they are not, then you will quickly become disheartened and give up, so ensure your immediate and intermediate goals are at an achievable level. For the longer-term goals you can aim higher. There are two reasons for this: first of all, just because something seems beyond your reach now, it doesn't mean that it always will be. Secondly, in five years' time you will have developed new skills, talents, qualifications, networks and so on, which will hopefully bring that higher goal much closer than it is now, thereby making it more achievable.

Bear in mind though, that your goals need to be realistic. There is no point setting the goal of becoming an opera singer if you sound like a frog in a bag every time you try to sing! You can't sell a talent or skill you don't have, no matter how many goals you make. Aim high by all means, but put the effort in to acquiring the skills you need to fulfill the highest goals achievable to *you*. Just because your best friend has achieved something doesn't mean that you too can reap the same rewards. It might not be the right path for you. Think carefully on this as you create your life map and set your goals, because they need to be personal to you, not influenced by anyone else. This is your life and your path—no one else's. Personal, achievable aspiration should be your watchwords.

CHAPTER FIVE:

Pyramid Power

A successful journey of self-transformation can only be made when you have a solid foundation on which to build. By this I mean that all your basic needs are being met. If they are not being met, then you will struggle to achieve your highest aspirations, because your mind will understandably be more focused on putting food on the table or paying your bills on time. That said, self-transformation can certainly help you to start meeting these basic needs more easily, so if your foundations are a little shaky right now, this chapter will show you exactly what you need to have in place, in order to create a solid baseline from which to build.

Maslow's Pyramid

In 1943, the US psychologist Abraham Maslow came up with a theory called the Hierarchy of Needs, which he illustrated using a pyramid shape, with our basic requirements at the bottom and the more aspirational needs towards the top. In moving through these tiers, people progress from surviving to thriving. However, should one or more of the lower levels of need be unmet, this deficiency greatly impairs personal progress, with the higher levels remaining unfulfilled.

At the pinnacle of this pyramid is the concept of self-actualization, which is the realization of one's full potential. Self-actualization is what we have been aiming for throughout this book. It is the realization of your goals, skills and talents, and the ability to transform your life, so that it fulfills you. Before you can truly master self-actualization, however, you must have your basic needs met. This gives you a very solid foundation upon which to build your dream life. Let's take a close look at Maslow's Hierarchy of Needs, so that you can identify any gaps that are holding you back, which you might need to address.

Self-actualization—We arrive at the pinnacle of the pyramid, which is the need to reach one's full potential and all that entails: creativity, the arts, appreciation of beauty, spontaneity, purpose, drive, ambition, aspiration, acceptance, problem-solving ability, resilience, robustness and freedom. To have reached this level is an indication that you are thriving and making your goals your reality. It also means that you have developed a strong ability to bounce back, so obstacles and challenges do not worry you too much, as you can solve problems easily and return stronger from the experience.

Esteem needs—We now move onto the fourth level, which is that of self-esteem—respect, accomplishment, talents, skills, achievements, confidence, image, a sense of autonomy and independence. Working on these contributes to a positive sense of self and overall confidence.

Social needs—The third level of need is that of social wellbeing: love, affection, inclusion, friendships, intimacy, a sense of belonging and connection. Humans are social creatures, so such connections are vital to our happiness.

Safety needs—The second level of need is that of safety and security, which includes financial stability, employment, positive family bonds, secure housing, good health and social stability. All these things in place add up to a deep sense of security.

Physiological needs—At the bottom of the pyramid are the very basic essentials for survival: air, food, water, shelter, warmth, clothing and rest. This is your baseline. If you are lacking anything in this area then you are in a dire situation, which must be addressed immediately.

Looking at the examples given for each tier of the pyramid, you should be able to quickly identify where there are obstacles to your progression. For instance, if you are currently out of work, then that represents a gap at the second level of need, and you will feel less safe and secure than if you had reliable employment and the income that goes with it. That being the case, adding "finding a job" to your immediate goals list will mean that you are aware of how this gap could hinder your progress—plus you are now committed to filling it in the next six months.

For self-transformation to occur, I would venture to suggest that the first three levels of Maslow's pyramid should be in place in your life. If they are not, then the first type of transformation you should make is to fill those gaps. There is little point dreaming of being a global business mogul if you currently don't know where your next meal is coming from. Get those basics in place first, before you move on to bigger things, because having gaping holes in those first three levels *will* prevent your progress.

As a qualified psychotherapist, I have used Maslow's pyramid many times to show clients where their attention needs to be, because this is what we mean when we say that someone has "fallen through the cracks". Often, they are unaware of the gaps in their lives and they are wondering why they feel so insecure or isolated. It's because their basic human needs are not being met.

TRANSFORMATIONAL TOOL: PYRAMID POWER

Take a piece of card and draw a large triangle on it. Divide the triangle into five sections, from bottom to top and name them after Maslow's model of needs, so physiological needs, safety needs, social needs, esteem needs and self-actualization. Bearing in mind any gaps you have identified, as we discussed above, colour in the levels you have already achieved. How does it look? Hopefully, at the very least, you will have been able to colour in the bottom level of basic physical needs.

The triangle will show you how much there is for you to do to achieve your full potential, and you can begin to progress through one level at a time as all your needs are met and you work your way up the pyramid. Cut out this triangle and keep it somewhere safe. Each time you feel that you have achieved a new level, colour in that section. In this way, you can see the progress that you are making. This exercise will help to keep you on track, showing you exactly where your focus ought to be and what you should be working on next to achieve a state of self-actualization and happiness.

A SPELL TO GET YOUR NEEDS MET

Moon phase: Full moon.

Items required: A white candle and holder, athame or carving tool, frankincense essential oil.

This candle ritual is designed to draw the things you need into your life. Only you will know what gaps you need to fill, so use a white candle which is suitable for all types of spells. Carve your need into the length of the candle with the athame. Use key words and phrases such as love, friendship or new job. Anoint the candle by rubbing the frankincense oil all over it. In magic, frankincense is often used as an attraction oil. Hold the candle in your hands and say:

> *"My need is genuine, my heart is true,*
> *I cast this spell and it comes through,*
> *I draw ------------- (state your need) to me,*
> *So I may live in harmony,*
> *So mote it be."*

Place the candle in the holder, light it and allow it to burn down naturally. Feel free to repeat the spell each full moon if you wish, as this will layer up the magic and aid in manifestation.

Set-Backs and Backslides

Life can be very unpredictable at times. Just because you have achieved the first three levels of Maslow's pyramid doesn't mean that you will always have all those bases covered. Jobs can be lost, relationships end, friendships turn sour and finances can be a bit up-and-down. In fact, life often throws a spanner in the works just when you think things are going well and you are about to achieve a big goal. It seems unfair and it can feel like an attack, but it's really not personal. You didn't do anything wrong. It's just part of the process. This is how your resilience, bounce-back and problem-solving abilities are honed.

Sometimes a set-back is actually a blessing in disguise. It could be that you didn't get that job because the company is actually in financial trouble and about to go under. It could be that your hot new date didn't show up because he was being arrested for a misdemeanour, or interrogated by the wife you didn't know he had! Such lucky escapes could be seen as a sign that the universe is actually protecting you.

Witches believe that there is a reason for everything and that includes the set-backs too. When something unexpected happens to derail your plans, it is usually because you were on the wrong path and something even better is coming along. A set-back frequently turns out to be a set-up, in that life is redirecting you to something else that will prove to be even more beneficial to you. You might lose your magazine column, but gain a book deal. Or lose a local job, just to be offered one in your dream location. Such things do happen, so try to have patience when it feels like you are being held back from an opportunity, as an even bigger one is usually waiting in the wings.

Backslides are also quite natural, though these are usually self-directed rather than as a result of unexpected events. A backslide tends to happen shortly after you've had some kind of break-through. It could be that things are going so well, you become complacent and stop putting as much effort into your goals, leading to a temporary pause on your progress. Suddenly your clients start dropping away, the work stops coming in or you fail an exam. This is life's little way of cracking the whip and telling you to keep putting the effort in. It's OK to have downtime, but don't allow yourself to backslide for too long. If you do, you might find that one of the levels of need that you thought you had nailed down suddenly requires your attention again. If that happens, go back to basics, work on filling those gaps and then press ahead.

CHAPTER SIX:

Living an Accomplished Life

In the past both men and women were expected to have certain accomplishments. Men were expected to be able to ride, shoot, fence, converse and uphold the rules of chivalry and gentlemanly conduct, while women would nurture gentler accomplishments such as sewing, painting, singing, playing a musical instrument, dancing, flower-arranging and so on. This might seem very old-fashioned to the modern mindset, but there is much to be said for the concept of spending time nurturing accomplishments, ambition and achievements.

Not only does achieving a goal feel good in the moment, it can help with your self-image and also how other people regard you too. Achievement boosts confidence and emboldens you to aim higher. It improves your capabilities. It garners respect from others. It teaches you that you *do* have what it takes to set and complete a task, be it large or small. Passing an exam, a driving test, graduating, learning how to swim or ice-skate—these are all valuable accomplishments, and they soon add up to define you as a multi-skilled individual. In this chapter we are going to explore what ambition and achievement means to you and how you can begin to lead an accomplished life.

Ambition vs Pipe Dreaming

Having ambition is one thing, but pipe dreaming is quite another—so how do you tell the difference? While ambition will move your life forward, pipe dreaming could actually hold you back. This is because an ambition is something that you are driven to do and it comes from within you. A pipe dream, however, is more likely to have been triggered by an external influence—for instance, you see your best friend publish a book and suddenly decide you want to be a writer. Or your sister has a baby and now you'd quite like one too. Pipe dreams come out of nowhere and might not be something you seriously thought about doing before. Furthermore, they can lead you away from your true path if you let them, as you spend time trying to keep up with the achievements of someone else, matching their goals, rather than achieving your own.

There is another kind of pipe dreaming to be aware of too, and that is when your skills don't match your dream. We touched on this earlier with the example of a tone-deaf opera singer. Trying to sell a talent you don't have is a complete waste of your time. Now, if you can hone that talent through tuition and qualifications, then it could become a legitimate ambition at some stage in the future, when you have gone through the training, but that might not always be possible. For example, you can't become a runway fashion model if you are very short, because you don't meet the usual height requirements and you can't change your stature. Therefore, this would be a pipe dream, not a realistic ambition (unless the fashion industry goes through a sea change).

The most successful ambitions are the ones where you have the talent to back them up and you are prepared to go through the training required to achieve them. This training could in itself become a part of your transformational journey. If your ambition is to become a nurse or a therapist, then you would need to commit several years of your life to completing a degree and the formal training required to qualify in such a profession. The important thing to bear in mind is that your ambitions must be self-directed, not dreams influenced by others.

Active vs Passive Involvement

To be in with any chance of achieving your ambitions, you need to make sure that you are an active participant in the process. Visualization does have its place in accomplishing any goal, but if it is all you ever do, you won't get very far. You must back up your visualizations and affirmations by taking action on your goals. Follow up on your ideas to see where they lead. Taking action can mean anything from signing up for a class, to sending an email, or researching your topic on the internet. You are the dynamo that can move your life forward, so be dynamic in your approach to self-transformation and start taking action. Use the following exercise to lay out the order of your ambitions.

TRANSFORMATIONAL TOOL: CREATE A LADDER OF ACHIEVEMENT

Take out the life map you created earlier and identify six or seven of your ambitions. They do not need to be related, but they need to be ones you are enthusiastic about beginning to achieve. Next, try to put them into some sort of order. It could be that one goal naturally leads onto another, but, if not, create an order in which you would like to achieve these goals. Now take a piece of card and draw a ladder. Make sure the ladder has as many rungs as you have ambitions, then write one ambition on each rung, writing the first you want to achieve on the bottom rung and working upwards. For example, if your goal is an academic one, you could name each rung of the ladder for a year of your degree, or name one for each level of education you plan to undertake, starting, perhaps, with a first degree and working up to a doctorate at the top of the ladder. In this way, you can see a clear path ahead of you, and you have wrestled the goals into some kind of logical sequence for you to follow. As you achieve each goal, colour it in to mark your progress and begin to work on achieving the next rung. This is the ladder of your success, so keep it somewhere safe so that you can refer back to it when you need to.

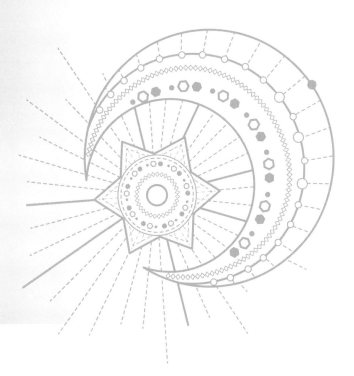

TRANSFORMATIONAL TOOL: FREE PLAY!

Free play is a term used by psychotherapists and refers to the act of self-directed play or amusement. Working on your accomplishments should be fun! It should not be a chore that you force yourself to do and, while any kind of achievement takes work, that doesn't mean that you can't have fun with it. So look at your life map and ladder of achievement, seek out the goal that seems the most fun and creative to you and set aside a specific amount of time to indulge in it. Make it a daily or weekly practice. You might set aside an hour a day to write, practise playing the piano, bake something, learn a language or exercise to music. You might take up meditation, learn more about spell-craft to hone your magical skills, or devise daily rituals that are geared toward achieving your goal, a step at a time. By factoring this type of free play into your day-to-day life, not only are you bringing your goal that much closer, you are also beginning to live a life of accomplishment—because all accomplishments take practice and the more you indulge in them, the more proficient you will become.

Creative Accomplishment and Mental Well-Being

Life can be very stressful at times, so having an accomplishment to work on can be a great form of stress relief. Arts, crafts, languages, culinary and baking skills, practising music, gardening, astronomy, model-making, playing sports and so on can all be used to take your mind off the stressful events of the day. So, in addition to your main self-transformation goals, you would be wise not to neglect your hobbies and the goals you made for them, as they will allow you to nurture your talents and explore your interests.

The benefits of having some kind of creative accomplishment to work on can't be overstated. It will give you a way to relax, offering a calming pastime when life gets hectic. Too often, busy people lose touch with their creative talents because they think that they don't have the time for them. You should *make* time for creative pursuits, for outdoor hobbies and sports, in the same way that you make time for your career and family. Hobbies are important because these accomplishments can help with conditions such as anxiety, ADHD, depression, PTSD and fatigue.

There is also a sense of achievement in having completed a creative project, be that a knitted scarf or a model aeroplane, or in playing well in a team sport such as football. It is wise to ensure that you have two hobbies to indulge in, one for indoors on a rainy day and another that gets you outside and meeting people. In this way, you will never be stuck for a way to relax and unwind, as you can always fall back on your hobbies, which in turn become accomplishments in their own right.

TRANSFORMATIONAL TOOL: CHOOSE YOUR HOBBIES

✦ Take up a favourite hobby that can be enjoyed indoors on dark winter's nights and dull rainy days. Gather the tools required and make a start on a new project.

✦ Think of a hobby or sport you might enjoy that will get you out and about in the fresh air. Join a sports team, take up walking, golf or horse riding. Book a lesson and make it part of your weekly or monthly routine.

Childhood Dreams Can Still Be Accomplished

Living an accomplished life depends on creating routines and habits that facilitate this. People are not born accomplished, any more than they are born literate. These are learned behaviours that come about by setting personal goals and challenges and by living each day with a creative spirit and a sense of adventure. Learn to think in terms of possibility, rather than limitation. Why shouldn't you play football in your fifties just as you did as a child? Why shouldn't you take up piano lessons or join a riding school, or dance class, if those are things you have always wanted to do? As adults, we have the autonomy to make our childhood dreams come true. Why waste that ability by telling yourself that you are too busy, too old, too poor or whatever?

All it takes is a small step forward for you to see that, actually, you can ride a horse and spend time at the stables, learn to play golf, or take up ballroom dancing. The world is full of opportunities and experiences, but you have to go out and grab them for yourself. Just because you can't afford to buy a horse of your own doesn't mean that you can't go riding each week. Just because you don't have a set of golf clubs doesn't mean that you can't borrow some and start taking lessons to learn the basics. Just begin where you are right now. Do whatever you can to take that first step towards your ideal accomplishment. This is how happiness is achieved and your inner child will thank you for it.

CHAPTER SEVEN

Stacking Up Advantages for Success

Self-transformation involves upskilling yourself. You need to be aware of what your skills are and where you need to improve them or fill in the gaps. Being a multi-skilled individual can open doors for you and bring about opportunities you never even dreamed of. Knowing how to define and sell your skills is also important. This kind of self-awareness will stack up the advantages in your favour, so that success begins to come to you more easily and frequently. While you will still need to work hard and you might experience set-backs, with a strong skill set under your belt, you are well equipped to keep moving forward.

Building a Skill Set

Having a set of skills works to your advantage because each skill you acquire will improve your overall capability. The more capable you are, the more adaptable you can be when circumstances change without warning, meaning that you can roll with the punches of life more easily. Life skills are vital in any self-transformation journey, regardless of what your ultimate goal might be. Looking for love? Communication skills will be required. Want greater independence? Financial skills will be essential. Need a new job? A driving licence can improve your chances of employment. Building up your skill set will stand you in good stead, no matter what your circumstances are, and it is a great foundation on which to improve your life. Below is a list of life skills that are very valuable indeed, but this is by no means exhaustive. How many of them do you have? How many others can you add?

✦ BOUNDARY SKILLS—knowing how to put up personal boundaries and how to protect them when someone oversteps the mark.

✦ COMMUNICATION SKILLS—especially listening, which is vital for all interactions.

✦ CONFLICT RESOLUTION AND DE-ESCALATION SKILLS—essential to achieve a win-win result or to calm a volatile situation. Knowing how to pick your battles is important.

✦ CULINARY SKILLS—knowing how to cook healthy meals from scratch—as well as being able to bake—means that you are aware of exactly what you are eating. Plus, you'll be well equipped to feed your family.

- DEBATING SKILLS—great for getting your point across, politely and without conflict.
- DOMESTIC SKILLS—knowing how to run and maintain a secure and comfortable home.
- DRIVING SKILLS—increase independence and improve job prospects. Everyone needs a getaway car at times!
- FINANCIAL SKILLS—understanding how credit works, how to create savings and how to budget your income can keep you out of unmanageable debt.
- FIRST AID SKILLS—vital if you have kids or care for someone, though useful for everyone as you never know when you might need this knowledge.
- FOREIGN LANGUAGE SKILLS—these improve job prospects and open doors to travel or working abroad.
- HOME REMEDY SKILLS—prevent visits to the doctor and save on prescription charges for common ailments such as coughs, colds and minor ailments.
- NAVIGATION SKILLS—essential if you want to travel alone. Don't rely on your satnav!
- RISK ASSESSMENT—vital for self-preservation, especially in unfamiliar territory.
- SELF-AWARENESS AND SELF-SOOTHING—know your triggers, your moods, your issues and have the ability to soothe yourself and take back control when any of the items on the list above rears its ugly head.
- SELF-DEFENCE SKILLS—great for confidence, feelings of safety and useful to have just in case.
- SOCIAL MEDIA SKILLS—understanding how social media can be used against you allows you to protect yourself accordingly. In addition, learning how to use it for networking, job searches, promoting a business and so on, can put you in a stronger position when it comes to success and is a positive way to build on your technology skills.
- SPIRITUAL SKILLS—meditation, prayer and communing with divinity are all useful for comfort, belief and existential explorations.
- TECHNOLOGY SKILLS—you don't need to be a whizz-kid, but you do need the basics.

These are just some of the life skills that can help to stack the advantages in your favour, especially when job hunting or seeking to make a major life change. Of course, you probably won't have all these skills in place right now, but I hope that the list serves to inspire you, because the more skills you have, the more well-rounded and self-sufficient you will become.

TRANSFORMATIONAL TOOL: PICK A SKILL, ANY SKILL

Look back over the list above and tick off all the skills you already have. Now pick out a new one that appeals to you and take steps to build it into your personal skill set. This could mean taking a First Aid course, or sending off for your provisional driving licence and booking a few lessons. Try to pick out a new skill which is in alignment with your main goal, or think of a skill not on the list, which you would need to have in order to move forward on your journey of change. Challenge yourself to learn one new skill a year and remember that we are all learning all the time, so when you have perfected a particular skill, add it to your skill-set list and be proud of yourself, even if it's only learning how to knit! Bear in mind, also, that some skills, such as cooking, can be self-taught, through trial and error, so there really is no excuse not to upskill yourself.

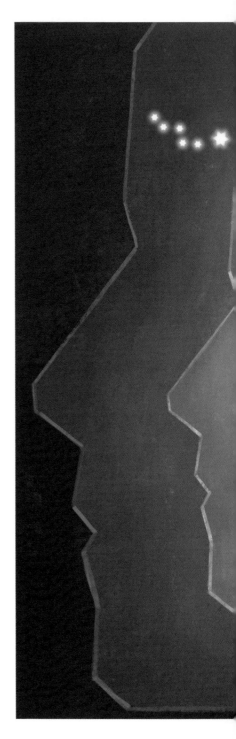

Selling Skills, Rather than Tasks

We all have skills and you probably have more of them than you are even aware of. Now you need to learn how to sell your skills. While this technique is most useful in the jobs market, it can be adapted to other situations too. In fact, turning your experiences into saleable skills is a valuable life skill in and of itself, so it is worth mastering.

All experiences in life can be broken down into a variety of skills and tasks. Take the stay-at-home mother, for instance, who is trying to get back into work. She might think that her experience of being at home for the past few years will stand in her way, but if she breaks down her day and sells the *skills*, rather than the *tasks*, she has a lot to recommend her. Her day might be a long round of nappy changes, school runs, preparing meals, housework, paying bills and entertaining the kids, but these are just the tasks she performs. The skills she is developing include:

- ✦ CARE SKILLS—looking after her children and anticipating their needs.
- ✦ TIME MANAGEMENT—she has to get the kids fed, dressed and in to school on time and be there to pick them up again.
- ✦ CULINARY SKILLS—she is making food for her family.
- ✦ DOMESTIC SKILLS—she provides a safe, clean and comfortable home.
- ✦ FINANCIAL SKILLS—paying bills on time and budgeting for the family.
- ✦ SOCIAL SKILLS—she adapts her methods of communication to suit her audience when she is entertaining her children.
- ✦ FIRST AID SKILLS—she is first on the scene for all those slips, trips and falls!
- ✦ SELF-AWARENESS SKILLS—she knows when she needs five minutes alone, when she is stressed and ready to snap at the kids.

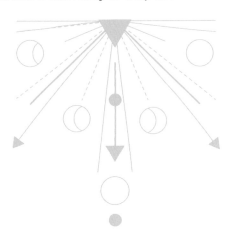

Extracting the skill from the task means that she now has quite a few saleable skills which will transfer well into a working environment. By listing her skills in this way, a prospective employer can see that she would be a valuable and capable member of the team and her job prospects improve. Viewing herself with this mindset is also likely to improve her self-esteem and feelings of accomplishment, not to mention giving a boost to her confidence. Now she can see what her advantages are, and how they can be stacked up and used in her favour.

Let's look at another example. A man who manages a fast food diner believes that his job is a dead end and that it does not prepare him for a better future. He goes to work each day, opening up the diner, peeling potatoes, prepping meals and so on. He might notice that they are low on meat and will need to put an order in to the supplier and promote a fish dish instead. He may also notice that they are low on small change in the till and he'll need to stop by the bank for more during his lunch break. At the end of the day, he banks up the takings and closes the diner. Just from these few tasks we can ascertain that he has developed the following transferable skills:

- **KEY-HOLDER RESPONSIBILITIES**—he opens up the fast food diner each day and locks up at night, ensuring the security of the building.
- **TIME MANAGEMENT**—he has to open up on time every day.
- **CULINARY SKILLS**—he is preparing food for the general public, adhering to food hygiene practices and standards.
- **PRODUCT AWARENESS AND PROMOTION SKILLS**—he knows what stock they have and what products to promote to ensure steady trade.
- **SOCIAL SKILLS**—he offers a friendly welcome to all his clients and good customer service.
- **FINANCIAL SKILLS**—he keeps a close eye on the till, replenishing it with change when needed, and accounting for and banking the day's takings.

Here you can see that far from being stuck in a dead-end job with no prospects, he is, in fact, developing some very useful skills that can easily be transferred to another form of employment. In selling these skills on his CV and in interviews, he can use them to his advantage to project his life forwards.

TRANSFORMATIONAL TOOL: EXTRACT THE LIFE SKILLS FROM YOUR LIFE EXPERIENCE

Think back over your own life experiences and responsibilities, whether they are professional, creative or family-orientated. What were your day-to-day tasks within that role or situation? What life skills were you developing during this time? What life skills are you developing in your current situation and how can you use these skills to help support your transformation? Remember to separate the skills from the tasks, bearing in mind that life skills are always transferable to other situations and environments. Add these skills to your list and continue to build on them, making sure that you update your CV with your transferable skills.

USING YOUR SKILLS FOR TRANSFORMATION

As you continue to build up a personal skill set, you will be making yourself more adaptable, capable and accomplished. In this way you can start to stack up advantages in your favour. Not all of your skills will be relevant to your transformational goal, but some of them will help to create the ideal structure for you to build your dream around. All skills are valuable and you never know when you might be called upon to use them. Learn to see the advantage in any situation. What can you learn from it? What can you take away from the experience? And how does it fit in with your overall ambitions and goals? Begin to regard yourself as a multi-skilled individual. If you happen across opportunities to learn something new, grab them with both hands and add to your skill set, to stack up your advantages for success.

CHAPTER EIGHT:

Break the Dream Apart

In order to make your dream come true, you must be brave enough to break it apart, examine it and know what you expect from it. What does achieving your dream give to you? How would it change your life and alter your daily routine? In what way is it beneficial? Transforming your life is possible, but you must be absolutely clear on what the pay-offs are going to be, otherwise you are likely to lose momentum or give up when things get hard. Remember your mission statement!

Some transformations are so big that they feel unattainable, but providing you have the talents, skills and knowledge to back up your goal, then any dream really can come true. That said, the bigger the goal, the easier it is to become completely overwhelmed by it, so you will need to break it apart to make it seem more manageable.

Achieving a transformational goal isn't always a linear process and sometimes you will need to circle round a few times before you begin to get anywhere. If your goal is to achieve a college qualification, for instance, but you do not have the minimum entry requirement to apply, then the first step would be to sign up for that course instead. Although this might seem like taking your dream a step backwards, you are really just laying a solid foundation on which to achieve the ultimate goal. Creating foundations are an important part of the process.

Begin with the End Result

So how do you go about turning a big transformation into reality? By breaking it down into bite-sized chunks, beginning with the end result that you want to achieve. So, if you wanted to become a novelist, the end result would be to have a published book in all the major bookshops. Working backwards from that point, we can see that you would need to achieve the following steps in order to attain the ultimate goal and transform yourself into a novelist:

✦ Published book on sale in bookshops = Novelist—goal achieved!

✦ Publisher accepts book and offers a contract.

✦ Literary agent submits book to publishers.

✦ Literary agent and author work on re-editing the book to publishing standards.

✦ Literary agent accepts manuscript and author for representation.

✦ Learn from rejections and adjust manuscript or approach.

✦ Send manuscript out to literary agents.

✦ Research possible literary agents and publishers.

✦ Edit and polish manuscript to the best of your ability.

✦ Review manuscript to final draft.

✦ Finish first draft of manuscript.

✦ Start writing novel.

✦ Set a manageable word count to write each day.

✦ Plan story and chapter outline.

✦ Have an idea for a novel.

Following these 15 steps can take you from the dream to the reality and it's the same technique with any goal. Though, as you can see, it can be a long process, so you will need patience and the fortitude to keep going.

TRANSFORMATIONAL TOOL: STEPPING STONES

Beginning with the end result of your chosen transformation, map out the stepping stones from that success, back to where you are now. Write this down as a list of steps. Break the dream into smaller chunks that you can achieve, one at a time. What needs to be put in place? Are there calls to make, emails to send, forms to fill out? Is there a new daily routine you need to set up, similar to the novelist in the above example meeting a daily word count? If so, then use the 66-Day Habit Tracker (see Chapter Four) to help you create that routine. Once you have traced back from the success of your goal to your current situation, count how many tasks there are—these are the stepping stones into your future. Make a start on working towards achieving the first step, then move on to the next, and so on. This is how dreams become reality.

The Fog

Sometimes, you just can't see your way ahead, no matter how hard you try. You might hit a wall that you just can't break through, or backslide so much that you lose all momentum. This seems to be something which occurs during any transformational journey or ambition. I call it the Fog, because it feels like you are surrounded by a thick mist that is obscuring the view of your chosen path. You do not know which way to turn and you remain stuck in one place.

Living through the Fog can be a scary time, particularly for those people who are very goal-orientated. It saps your motivation and enthusiasm; it drains your energy and clouds your optimism with doubt. It puts the brakes on progress, at least for a time. From knowing exactly where you were heading, ticking off goals as you went, suddenly you feel stuck, trapped and stagnant. The Fog can also take things away from you—jobs, relationships, friends. They all seem to fade away, out of focus, dim and distant, leaving you alone and searching for the way forward. It can feel very isolating.

But the Fog has a purpose—for, behind the grey curtain of mist, the universe is setting up your future, putting things in place that you can't see right now, but which will reveal themselves to you in due course. It is stripping away all those things that no longer serve you, making space in your life for something better to come along. In the Fog, magic is happening—you just can't see it.

TRANSFORMATIONAL TOOL: ENDURING THE FOG

Make no mistake about it, the Fog is a real test of your endurance! Living through such a time in your life can be quite tough, but there are things that you can do to make it easier to bear.

✦ Check in with yourself. Have you been indulging in any self-sabotaging behaviour? If so, rectify it immediately.
✦ Count your blessings. Make a mental list of all the things you have going for you.
✦ Demonstrate gratitude for all the good people and things in your life right now.
✦ Clear your space with a block-blasting spell (see opposite).
✦ Believe! All those things you have been doing to transform your life up to this point are preparing to manifest.
✦ Have faith that good things will come to you again.
✦ Keep up with your visualizations and affirmations.
✦ Practice self-care.
✦ Keep going!

A SPELL TO BLAST THROUGH BLOCKS

Moon phase: Best performed during a waning dark moon.
Items required: A large plate, a sticky note, a black pen, two lavender or pine incense sticks.

This is a classic uncrossing spell to blast away anything that is holding you back. Take all the items to a quiet place where you will not be disturbed. Using the black pen, write these words on the sticky note: "I blast all blocks from my life." Stick the note on the underside of the plate. Sit for a time and think of all the blocks being cleared from your path. Imagine the Fog lifting, so that you can see your way ahead once more. Then light the incense sticks for their cleansing energies and lay them on the plate in the form of a St Andrew's cross. Leave them in place until they have burned to ash, then scatter the ashes to the four winds to complete the spell.

Set the Date

One key component of all manifestation and transformation magic is that you must commit to a date by which you will have achieved your goal. This puts a time frame on your intention. It will also help to keep you on track with your progress, as you will know exactly how many stepping stones you still have to cross before the deadline looms, which increases a sense of urgency and motivation.

A manifestation date isn't set in stone. In fact, if you are doing this for the first time, you might need to adjust your date several times. This isn't a sign of failure; it simply means that you are learning how to set realistic dates in alignment with your goals. Your chosen date should not be so far away that you have no emotional attachment to it, but nor should it be so soon as to be unrealistic. For example, imagine you wanted to leave a job that makes you unhappy. Setting a date three years away could lead to feelings of depression as it means you will be in your current job for all that time. On the other hand, setting a date for next week is quite unrealistic too, as you probably will not have found a new position in just seven days! A date somewhere in between—say, in 18 months' time—is much more realistic. Your date should be achievable, but not years and years ahead. The more you practise attaching manifestation dates to your intentions, the better you will be. In time, you will come to know what you can achieve and when.

TRANSFORMATIONAL TOOL: COMMIT TO A DATE

Take out your list of stepping stones. Think carefully about how long it will take for you to achieve each step. Set a date for the first two steps, making them relatively soon. Now think about when you would like to achieve your ultimate goal and write that date in too. Bear in mind that this final date could be subject to change, as you work your way through the steps. Having an end date in mind, however, will keep you motivated to meet the deadline. As soon as you have achieved the first two stepping stones, set dates for the next two and so on, until you have reached your transformational goal. Bear in mind that some later steps might be achieved first and that is OK. This goes back to what we were saying earlier about ambitions not being a linear journey. Be thankful for the jump-start, but keep working on the foundational steps too. Remember, foundations are important—don't skip them!

SELF-REGULATED PROGRESS

When no one is cracking the whip or commanding you to do things, it can be easy to lose motivation. You should therefore use the techniques in this chapter to self-regulate your progress. In a way, your journey of self-transformation is one long act of self-regulation. You have observed what needs to change, set the ultimate goal, altered your behaviour to be in alignment with that goal and you are now at the stage where you need to reinforce your patterns and monitor your progress. You are doing great, so stick with it!

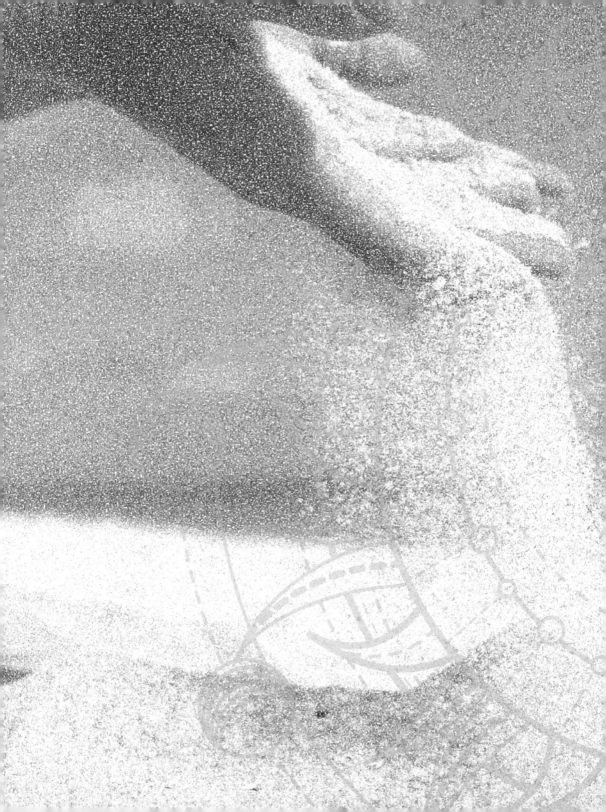

CHAPTER NINE:

Let the Transformation Begin!

Making any kind of fresh start is always an exciting time. Your levels of optimism are usually high, you can see a brighter future ahead of you and your happiness is increased, because you are taking control of your life and forging ahead with your plans for what you want. Sometimes, though, you need to get out of your own way. By this, I mean that, while your visualizations should be detailed, you should not be so rigid in your approach that you fail to recognize a manifestation, simply because it differs somewhat from your dream.

There are times when the universe will give you exactly what you asked for, but it won't look like you imagined. Often it will be even better—something beyond your imagining. Occasionally, though, it can appear to be so mundane that you reject it without thought and the manifestation slips through your fingers, right when it was within your grasp. If this happens, learn from it and continue to manifest your goal, working on your transformation so that when you are given a second chance, and you will be, you can grab onto it with both hands, even if it comes in a guise you didn't expect.

DON'T LET PRIDE GET IN THE WAY

If you have been working towards something for a while and an opportunity comes up, then of course you should take it. However, some people refuse these opportunities because they imagined an immediate leap to the heights of success, while the opportunity they are offered is less glamourous. For example, it's great that you want to transform yourself into a best-selling novelist, but don't turn down the chance to write a monthly piece for the website of your child's school. Turning down the smaller manifestations can block the bigger ones from coming your way, and looking down your nose at them as not being good enough for you will derail your plans. Snobbery has no place in manifestation! Keep in mind that transformation can be a slow process and that a less glamorous opportunity can be the start of something. It's all about getting your foot in the door, so accept the opportunity, commit to the work with enthusiasm and be grateful for it.

TRANSFORMATIONAL TOOL: VOLUNTEER

You should also consider volunteering in a way that supports your transformational goal. Writing gratis for a magazine gets you a byline and helps you to begin creating a network of editors. Reading books for a publisher and reviewing them on your blog gets your name known by editors in those publishing houses. Volunteering as a call-handler for a helpline can assist in your goal to become a counsellor, teacher or nurse. Walking dogs will never make you rich, but it could be the first step towards becoming a vet or veterinary nurse. The same is true for volunteering with an animal shelter or charity.

Have a think about what volunteering opportunities there might be, which are a small step towards your transformational goal and start making some calls, offering your time. This will put you on the edge of the life you want to lead, allowing you a taste, to see if it is really something you want to pursue. As a bonus, you get to do your bit for society too.

A SPELL FOR A LUCKY BREAK

Moon phase: Perform during a waxing moon.

Items required: A gold candle and holder, ylang-ylang essential oil.

Sometimes all you need is the right person to come along and see your potential, offering you a lucky break and assisting in your transformation. To draw this kind of lucky break towards you, anoint a gold candle with ylang-ylang oil to attract positive opportunities, light it and repeat the following chant nine times, out loud or in your head, before letting the candle burn down naturally,

"A lucky break I seek to find,
It comes to me through space and time,
I call this opportunity,
I'll know it when it comes to me."

SUCCESS IS A NATURAL RESULT OF TRANSFORMATIVE THINKING

Once you accept that success is natural and that you have every right to your fair share of it, the achievements will begin to come thick and fast. This is because success is a natural consequence of transformative thinking. Throughout this book you have been training your mind to think in terms of possibility and make the most of your skills. This will naturally draw positive things your way, because like attracts like.

Life is not meant to be a constant struggle. While there will undoubtedly be ups and downs, a life of endless strife is an indication that something is out of alignment. It could be your habits, your mindset or your self-sabotaging behaviours, but something is working against you, and it is often something which is in your own control. Identifying what it is, and addressing it, means that success will begin to come your way again, slowly at first and then more quickly. This is because success has a snowball effect. A small win leads to a bigger win, which leads to an accomplishment, which in turn leads to the achievement of a goal. Reaching one goal makes you realize that you can fulfill others too, and so one success rapidly leads on to the next and the next, and so on. Success is natural and you can experience it as many times as you set a goal and commit to achieving it.

Indifference to Your Success

There will inevitably be people around you who are indifferent to your goals and your success. Don't take this personally. Most people are wrapped up in their own lives and they might be too busy working on their own transformation to give a hoot about yours! That's OK. You don't need cheerleaders. You have the power to motivate yourself and to get ahead under your own steam.

Bear in mind that no one else can see the future you envision for yourself, no matter how much you might want them to, or how often you describe it to your loved ones. They might wish you well, but they can't *see* your goal—at least not in the way that you can. They can only see the current surface-level of your life and they will interact with you and form their judgements, based on that alone. They might even scoff at your goals. Again, that's OK. While it's not very nice (and you might need to change your friends!) just think of how foolish they will seem when you have achieved what you set out to do. They might even try to emulate your success, because as the saying goes, "first they laugh, then they copy".

Indifference can be quite hurtful, especially when it comes from someone very close to you. You might have chosen a goal that your family's values do not align with—refusing to join the family business in favour of striking out on your own, for instance. In such a situation, you will need to moderate your expectations of the amount of support they will give to your transformational journey. In addition, recognising when someone is showing indifference can help to keep things in perspective, because if you know where their behaviour is coming from, you can dial down your expectations of their support and prepare yourself for the snub. Here are some common behaviours which demonstrate indifference.

+ Turning away from you when you refer to your plans.
+ Changing the subject when you mention your goals.
+ Refusing to discuss the changes you want to make.
+ Becoming very absorbed in something else whenever the subject comes up.
+ Turning up the television or music loudly when you have a success to share.
+ Leaving the room or walking away.
+ Choosing to interact with the children or pets instead of you.
+ Whispering behind your back.
+ Non-verbal signs of irritation such as sighing, huffing, arm-folding and eye-rolling.
+ Refusing to engage, or engaging passively, when you try to show them something you've achieved, such as academic certificates, wedding photos or your recently published article.
+ Passive-aggression, such as barbed "jokes" about your fresh start or new image.

- Sabotaging behaviours designed to derail your success, such as not passing on messages, "accidentally" deleting emails or shredding work.
- Trying to set themselves up as your rival i.e. applying for the same promotion.
- Malice—this goes beyond indifference and means that someone is actively working against you. They might make calls to your new boss with a made-up complaint, or actively spread rumours about you which are untrue. Take them to task and nip this in the bud immediately!

TRANSFORMATIONAL TOOL: DEALING WITH INDIFFERENCE

First of all, try not to take these kinds of behaviour personally. It's really not about you—it's about them. For some reason, your actions and goals have triggered something in them and they are acting out accordingly. It might be fear, envy or spite, but your plans have activated a certain response in them, one which they know is unfair and unkind, so they show indifference, rather than revealing their true emotions. Go back to "Who Keeps You Small" in Chapter Three. Nine times out of ten, the people who show indifference belong under this heading. If this is someone you are very close to, you will need to gently confront them and ask why they want to hold you back. If they are people you see only occasionally, then you might want to consider ending that relationship altogether. You don't need their negativity weighing you down and trying to hold you back, or keep you in your place. You are entitled to succeed in your own life—how other people emotionally respond to that success is not your responsibility.

TRANSFORMATIONAL TOOL: INVEST IN YOURSELF

Investing in your transformation is one of the most powerful things you can do to aid the manifestation of your goal. Now I'm not saying that you should spend all your money, but a modest investment here and there is a fantastic affirmation of action. This could mean buying a new outfit for a job interview, or buying a new computer for your plans to build a graphic design business. It might mean buying the gear you need to take up your dream hobby, or investing in a storage system for your proposed e-commerce handicrafts business. Whatever your goal might be, make a plan to treat yourself to a little something that you know you will need once you are living your transformed life—be that a fancy pen or laptop to write a book, an item of clothing that represents who you want to be, or a new lawnmower to landscape gardens. Make that purchase, in accordance with your budget, and invest in yourself.

CHAPTER TEN:
Self-Actualization

Reaching a state of self-actualization means that you are regularly achieving your goals and living something of a charmed life. Self-actualized people tend to be independent, grounded, compassionate, creative, high achievers, friendly, honest, joyful, ethical, honourable, optimistic and forward-thinking. They are not perfectionists or martyrs to their cause. They do not bear malice to those who are more successful than they are, instead they use them as inspiration. They enjoy their life and create new experiences for themselves. They try to help people when they can, but they will not take on undue responsibility for the burdens and issues of others. They don't carry the weight of the world on their shoulders.

Signs of Change

So, how do you know if you have reached a place of self-actualization and transformation? Sometimes people can be so caught up in the mechanics of transforming their lives that they miss the signs that the change is about to occur, or has already happened. Here are some common signs that the change you want is about to manifest.

✦ A feeling of contentment.
✦ A lack of anxiety—you know it's coming, so why worry?
✦ Having dreams that you already have what you want.
✦ Similarly, experiencing dreams that you are living your ideal life.
✦ When there's a test from the universe, such as a temporary set-back or backslide, you rise to the challenge with grace. It means you're close, so don't give up!
✦ A strong sense of gratitude for everything you already have.
✦ Other people start to remark and comment on the change in you.
✦ New habits feel natural.
✦ You are generally feeling more optimistic.
✦ Strangers respond to you differently, in a positive way.
✦ Your aura feels bright and shiny!
✦ Your outlook on life is generally a lot more positive.

TRANSFORMATIONAL TOOL: WHAT DOES YOUR VICTORY LOOK LIKE?

You need to know exactly what the victory of your transformation will look like. If you don't recognize victory when it happens, you can exhaust yourself working for something which you already have and didn't recognize! That would result in burnout. So make sure that you hold a clear objective in your mind of how your personal victory appears. Will it be reaching a particular weight, not smoking for six months or longer, being happy in a new job, rebooting your image or being in a healthy, loving relationship? Knowing when you have achieved your objective means that you are ready to set the next goal. Now you can start working on that instead, while maintaining the habits and behaviours that helped you to achieve your initial objective. In this way you can transform your whole life.

TRANSFORMATIONAL TOOL: CELEBRATE!

It is amazing how many people neglect to celebrate their victories and successes, but celebration is important because it acknowledges what you have achieved. It is a way to give yourself a pat on the back for a job well done. Your celebrations don't need to be large and extravagant if you don't want them to be. A quiet gathering with family and friends to celebrate your new business deal or work promotion is sufficient. Buy a cake and a few balloons and have a little party! You've earned it.

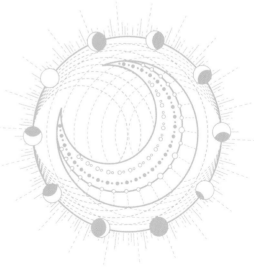

RESPECT WHERE YOU HAVE COME FROM

Respecting your past is just as important as celebrating your current success. This is because when you honour your past, you are either forgiving or celebrating your past self and the things they brought to the table. If you have had a difficult past, that makes it all the more remarkable that you have succeeded up to this point in your life. You did it! In spite of everything and everyone that was against you. Honour the journey that you have been on and look forward to the next stage.

Reflecting on your past can be quite a momentous experience, as you may realize just how far you have come. You might feel like a completely different person to the one you were back then. Then again, you might realize that you miss aspects of your old self and determine to revive them in your current life. Taking a trip down memory lane is a useful tool of self-awareness. Whatever your past looks like, it helped to shape who you are today. It allowed you to develop resilience, robustness and fortitude. It gave you skills and experiences that you can build upon for a better future. Honour your past and the person you used to be, for their footsteps brought you to this point in your life.

MANIFESTATION CAN FEEL SURREAL

When you have been working on a big goal for a long time and it suddenly manifests in your life, it can all feel quite surreal. This is normal. Change, when it finally happens, tends to happen quickly. It snowballs. Something you once regarded as a dream is now your reality and the truth is it will probably take some time for you to adjust to that fact. Perhaps you can barely dare to believe that it just happened, because you fear that it will all be snatched away again, leaving you back at square one. This is a natural fear, but usually one which is unfounded.

For a large transformation to occur, you will have had to change your entire way of thinking and behaving. Once your mindset has been changed for the better, you are unlikely to go back to those old negative ways of thinking that might sabotage your success. New habits are no longer new, they are automatic and the resulting transformation is a natural consequence of this change in your behaviour.

However, the surreal feeling can be quite unnerving, even spooky, at times. It's as if you are living in a dream—and you are! Manifestation is *your* dream made real.

The transformation you imagined has come true. It's the "pinch me" moment we often hear about, when everything just falls into place and your goal is now your day-to-day life. Try not to get too spooked by it. Enjoy the results of your journey, for they are the natural product of your own hard work. Show gratitude for what you have achieved and start making plans for the next transformation!

Conclusion

A Changeling is Born!

I hope that you have enjoyed this book and that you have found the guidance, tools, spells and information presented here useful. The desire for change is a natural aspect of personal growth. You should never feel guilty for wanting something different from what you already have, or for hoping to better your life in some way. Self-improvement is the mark of an enlightened individual who is both self-aware and proactive.

Within this book you have learned all the steps required to bring about positive change in your life. You have all the tools you need to go forward and make those changes happen, starting today. With your mission statement, life map, pyramid of needs, ladder of achievement, stepping stones plan and your unique set of skills, you can begin to forge the kind of life you really want.

You are a self-fulfilling prophecy, a changeling reborn and you can shapeshift whenever you want, using the science of change, magical spells and the psychotherapy concepts we have explored in these pages. All you have to do now is to decide who and what you want to be. Let the transformation begin!

I wish you great joy and success for your future, changeling, until our next merry meeting.

Serene blessings,

Marie Bruce x

Further Reading

Books by Marie Bruce

Celtic Spells (Arcturus, 2022)

Moon Magic Card Deck (Arcturus, 2022)

The Book of Spells (Arcturus, 2022)

Wicca (Arcturus, 2022)

Other books on Magic and Witchcraft

Buckland, Raymond, *Buckland's Complete Book of Witchcraft,* Llewellyn, 1997

Cunningham, Scott, *Wicca: A Guide for the Solitary Practitioner,* Llewellyn, 1997

Cunningham, Scott, *Living Wicca: A Further Guide for the Solitary Practitioner,* Llewellyn, 1997

Cunningham, Scott, *The Truth About Witchcraft Today,* Llewellyn, 1997

Curott, Phyllis, *Book of Shadows: A Modern Woman's Journey into the Wisdom of Witchcraft and the Magic of the Goddess,* Piatkus, 1998

Davis, Owen, *The Oxford Illustrated History of Witchcraft & Magic,* Oxford University Press, 2017

De Pulford, Nicola, *Spells & Charms,* Godsfield Press, 1999

Greenleaf, Cerridwen, *The Practical Witch's Spellbook: For Love, Happiness and Success,* Running Press, 2018,

Guiley, Rosemary Ellen, *The Encyclopaedia of Witches and Witchcraft,* Facts on File, 1989

Horne, Fiona, *Witch: A Magickal Journey – A Guide to Modern Witchcraft*, Thorsons, HarperCollins, 2000

Hutton, Ronald, *The Triumph of the Moon: A History of Modern Pagan Witchcraft*, Oxford University Press, 1999

Illes, Judika, *The Element Encyclopedia of Witchcraft: The Complete A–Z for the Entire Magical World*, Element, Harper Collins, 2005

Illes, Judika, *The Element Encyclopedia of 5000 Spells: The Ultimate Reference Book for the Magical Arts*, Element, Harper Collins, 2004

Kane, Aurora, *Moon Magic: A Handbook of Lunar Cycles, Lore, and Mystical Energies*, Quarto Publishing Group, 2020

Jordan, Michael, *Witches; An Encyclopedia of Paganism and Magic*, Kyle Cathie, 1998

Moorey, Teresa, *Spells & Rituals: A Beginner's Guide*, Hodder & Stoughton, 1999

Moorey, Teresa, *Witchcraft: A Beginner's Guide*, Hodder & Stoughton, 1996

Moorey, Teresa, *Witchcraft: A Complete Guide*, Hodder & Stoughton, 2000

Morningstar, Sally, *The Wicca Pack: Weaving Magic into your Life*, Godsfield Press, 2001

Morningstar, Sally, *The Wiccan Way*, Godsfield Press, 2003

Saxena, Jaya and Zimmerman, Jess, *Basic Witches: How to Summon Success, Banish Drama, and Raise Hell with Your Coven*, Quirk Books, 2017

Van de Car, Nikki, *Practical Magic: A Beginner's Guide to Crystals, Horoscopes, Psychics, and Spells*, Running Press, 2017